D1404038

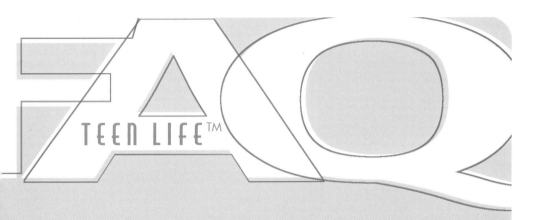

TEEN LIFE™

FREQUENTLY ASKED QUESTIONS ABOUT

When a Friendship Ends

Judith Levin

ROSEN
PUBLISHING®

New York

Published in 2008 by The Rosen Publishing Group, Inc.
29 East 21st Street, New York, NY 10010

Library of Congress Cataloging-in-Publication Data

Levin, Judith (Judith N.), 1956–
Frequently asked questions about when a friendship ends /
Judith Levin.
    p. cm.—(FAQ: teen life)
Includes bibliographical references and index.
ISBN-13: 978-1-4042-1936-6 (library binding)
ISBN-10: 1-4042-1936-6 (library binding)
1. Friendship in adolescence. 2. Interpersonal relations in
adolescence. I. Title.
BF724.3.F64L48 2007
158.2'5—dc22

                                                    2007004120

Manufactured in the United States of America

Contents

Introduction

As children, we're taught to sing: "Make new friends, but keep the old. One is silver and the other gold." The words remind us to stay open to meeting new people, but not to give up too easily on a tried-and-true pal. They also remind us not to turn our backs on childhood friends as we make new friends in high school.

It's good advice—but it's not advice you can always follow. We can't always keep old friends. Life gets in the way: friends outgrow each other. They move away. They go to different schools, or end up in different academic tracks than you. They change in different ways, and move on to new friends. Sometimes friends betray you (or you betray them), and it is not possible to repair the damage that has been done. You may realize that you just don't like each other anymore. Or your friend deserts you, and you don't even know why.

Some friends drift apart. You grow up from partners on the seesaw, develop separate interests as you mature, and now are content just to wave when you see each other.

Other friends part with anger, tears, and pain. The loss of a friend can be terrible. The friend who was like your sister or brother, who was by your side since almost before you can remember, is suddenly looking at you as if you don't exist. You're suddenly not cool enough, you listen to the wrong music, or something.

We often share our most memorable experiences with our friends, which is why losing a close companion is like losing a part of ourselves.

"What's the big deal?" someone might ask as you mourn your lost friend. After all it's "only" a friend. It's not a family member or someone with whom you've had a romance. But it's not "only" a friend. The experiences you went through together are memorable, and friendship is special.

What Is a Friend?

A friend is someone you know, like, and trust. But there's more to friendship: just trusting and liking each other isn't enough. You both have to want to be friends.

Here's something else important about what friends are: some of the best ones feel like family, but you weren't born into a friendship. You're pretty much stuck with the family you're born into, but you can choose your friends. This also means you (or your friend) can unchoose a friendship, which can be a good or a bad thing. You're not stuck with each other forever if you don't want to be, which is great. It feels bad, though, if you and a friend have a falling out, and you may not have a chance to put the relationship back together again.

That said, you are in a relationship with a friend, just as you are with a family member or a romantic partner—even though they're different kinds of relationships. You'll probably move away from home and your family eventually. You may move into and out of romantic involvements, especially during your teen years. You'll probably leave some friendships, too. If you succeed in finding and keeping a lifelong friend or two, those people will be there for you (and you for them) when you leave home, get together and break up with your sweeties, and go through the changes and stresses of becoming an adult.

There are many relationships that have a natural lifespan. You will meet various people, share time and experiences, and part. That's normal. That also means that for many relationships in your life, there will come a time when you want them to be less important—or you will have to bear the pain of somebody else telling you that your friendship is less important to him or her.

WHAT DOES IT TAKE TO BE A FRIEND?

Friendship offers some obvious benefits: company (even if you like being alone, you probably don't like it all the time), fun, and a person with whom you can be yourself without worrying too much if you sound like a jerk. Friends are people you've chosen because you like one another, so that when you're feeling down about yourself, they can remind you that you're not so bad. They can be a safety net as you walk the tightrope of high school uncertainties and difficulties. Friendship also offers glimpses into other people's lives. If you spend any time with a friend's family, you get to see what other families are like and get more perspective on yours. In comparison to your friend's brother, maybe yours isn't so bad. If your parents fight a lot, maybe it's helpful to hear that other parents do, too— or that they don't, so that you can imagine being in a marriage someday that is more companionable and happy than the one your parents have.

A friendship may offer more comfort and safety than a romance. It's easier to be reasonable about what you expect from friends—you know they're not perfect and you don't need them to be—while it is all too easy in romances to imagine that you're going to find the one magic person to fulfill your every need. You're less likely to expect "and they lived happily ever after" from a friend. Certainly you hope that friendships last, but you're less likely to interpret every argument as "you don't love me anymore."

Kinds of Friendships

When you were little, you may have had neighborhood friends or you were friends with the kids of your parents' friends. They may still be your best friends. Or they may have been important in your life when you were younger, but the friends who are closer to you now might be the ones you picked, not those who entered your life through circumstance.

Sharing Interests

There are friendships based on sharing a common interest: your friends on the baseball team, student council, or from the orchestra. You might be part of a crowd that gets together to trade old comic books or take photographs. Your common interest ties you together. You wouldn't be friends if you didn't have something in common. It could be something obvious. You each

Friendships are often formed because of the interests each person shares. Sharing interests allows friends to spend enjoyable time together.

care intensely about something that requires a lot of work (competitive swimming for one person and violin for the other) and get together to watch old movies after your hours of daily practice. Or your connection might be less obvious: you could share similar values or have the same sense of humor.

Having common ground doesn't mean you have to be the same or like the same things. A good friend can introduce you to something you never would have discovered on your own. You have your friendship in common, you have chosen to dedicate yourselves to it, and you like being together.

Sharing Circumstances

There may be people you choose to chat with at school or work, though you don't see one another outside that setting. You like each other OK. Your conversations make geometry class or the time behind the counter at the coffee shop easier to bear, but you're not going to tell them about the person you're secretly in love with or how worried you are about your parents' arguments.

These are mostly casual friends, acquaintances, but they still have a role in your life. You can be comfortable with them. If they are friends from work or a hobby group, you may have a chance to be friends with people older or younger than you. Friends a few years or a few decades older than you provide a glimpse into the world of adults—not parents, but just adults as people. Friends a bit younger can give you a chance to be the "adult" and the expert—quite a relief from being someone's kid or someone's student.

Sharing Secrets

Other friends are close friends—more like the dictionary definition that includes liking, knowing, and trusting. This might be a best, joined-at-the-hip-since-grade-school friend who's like your twin. It might be a small group of friends whose members manage to be equally close. Or it could be a big group of friends. Generally, if the group gets big, the friendships become more casual. It's probably not realistic to expect your most personal secret to be safe if you tell fifteen out of twenty people in the group. After all, if you're telling fifteen people, how private is it?

What a Good Friendship Takes

What makes someone a good friend? What do you have the right to look for? What should he or she offer?

Respect and Acceptance

Friends might say you've talked enough about how badly you did on the history test and suggest that you all go take a walk or eat pizza to make you feel better. They do not say, "Yawn," or tell you you're an idiot for caring about a grade (or an idiot for not being better at history). When you talk about something that matters, friends do not roll their eyes, smirk at one another over your head, or make you feel bad about yourself. Friends are slow to judge. (They might tease, but they don't make you feel terrible about yourself!)

The best of friends respect and admire one another. They also feel comfortable enough together to share their secrets.

Honesty and Loyalty

There's a Sicilian proverb that says, "Only a friend will tell you when your face is dirty." Honest isn't the same as mean, however. A friend won't scream that you have a dirty face in homeroom. Friends will tell you if they're worried about you, mad at you, or mad about something else. They may tell you if they think the person you've chosen to fall in love with is going to lead you into serious trouble, but they will support you in your decisions and keep the "I told you so's" to a minimum if he or she breaks your heart.

A note about honesty: people differ about how much they want to talk about. Some want to "process" everything. Others don't. Friends come to some understanding about this. Feeling free to be yourself with your friends means not being forced to violate your own sense of what it is OK to talk about, just as people should feel free among their friends to dress and think as they like. With your closest friends, you should feel that it would be safe to talk about most everything. Friends should like the real you (and you should feel the same way). When you disagree, you can argue about it and know that you're clearing the air and your argument will pass. That's part of friendship, too.

Discretion

At its most basic, discretion means that friends keep each other's secrets. Friends don't blab. Also, friends use their judgment about what to tell, even if they haven't been sworn to secrecy.

This rule has an important exception: If the secret is life-threatening or life-endangering, then friends get help for each other. If someone is being physically abused, is talking about suicide, is hurting his or her own body, or is suggesting that collecting guns and using them is a way to solve a problem, then you enlist the professional help of a counselor, teacher, or other adult. You tell a friend's secret if someone is in danger.

Support

Support is something like "being there" for your friends when they need it. It's also being there when they're really happy about something. Of course, friends get jealous of each other sometimes, but you don't let your disappointment take away your friends'

Though we should enjoy the company of those we choose to be our good friends, close relationships carry a lot of responsibility, such as companionship and trust.

happiness. Your friends, in return, do not rub your nose in their triumphs. This is where it helps to know that honesty doesn't always mean "the truth, the whole truth, and nothing but the truth." You owe your best friend a certain amount of tact and discretion, or the friendship may be severely stressed.

Friendship Isn't Easy

Friendship asks a lot from people, but it also gives a lot. You are asking for and offering trust, confidentiality, companionship, honesty, support, and a willingness to think of what someone else needs, not just what you need.

But that's a demanding list. Suppose you actually think your friend is becoming a jerk? Suppose she can't keep a secret? Suppose one of you gets the nod from someone in the "in" crowd? Suppose you grow and change? Well, the last one is going to happen for sure. Can this friendship survive?

two

WHY DO FRIENDSHIPS END?

Friendships form in different ways. Sometimes there is the instant recognition that someone is meant to be in your life. Other times you learn slowly to like someone and enjoy his or her company. Friendship can be as mysterious as falling in love. There is chemistry to it, and you can't always explain why one person becomes a friend and someone else doesn't. You might just "click" with someone who's very different from you.

Friendships end in different ways, too. People grow apart little by little—or the friendship may end with explosions, anger, and bad feelings that are hard to get over. Maybe one of you truly did something unforgivable. Maybe it was a misunderstanding, but so many angry words passed between you that your friendship is damaged beyond repair. Or a friend ends the friendship, sometimes suddenly.

It's natural that as you grow older, you may no longer see eye-to-eye with friends you were once close to.

Ten Great Questions to Ask Someone You Trust About Friendships

1 What should I do if my friend's in danger, but makes me promise to keep it a secret?

2 Does my friend's dumping me mean I'm no good?

3 I'm feeling so bad about losing my friend—will I ever feel happy again?

4 How can I meet new people?

5 What can I do about a clingy friend?

6 How do I know if it's time to end a friendship that's become painful to me?

7 How can I separate myself a little from an old friend I've outgrown?

Is it OK to put my friendships on the back burner because I would rather spend time with my sweetie?

If my friend gets really angry at me, does that mean she doesn't like me anymore?

How can I tell my friend that we need to change some things about our friendship?

When a Person Changes

Much of what challenges friendships starts with change. You or your friend change interests. It could be a change in religious beliefs ("I've decided to keep kosher, and I can't eat at your house or the food court anymore"); sexual orientation ("You're what?"); or a new set of life goals ("No one in this neighborhood goes to college. What're you, a snob?", "The army? You want to kill people or something?").

Family events or personal tragedies can challenge friendships. If a friend's family became much poorer or much richer, or if a parent went to jail or became famous, how would it affect the friendship? What if a friend became terribly ill or was injured and needed a wheelchair? Of course, people want to believe that they would equally rejoice in their friends' luck and support them in their troubles, and that friends would do the same for them, but sometimes it's hard.

What all these scenarios have in common is that change can be threatening to friendships. Change scares people because they can't predict or control how a friend will change, how much he or she will change, and how much will stay the same about a friendship. There is a chance that a changing person might no longer value the friendship in its current state. But many changes do not have to mean an end to the friendship. The friendship might just need to be adjusted a little.

Cliques

In high schools across the country, students separate into groups based on their interests, what they wear, where they hang out, and common activities. Other times they are identified by the color of their skin or their families' economic class. These groups are commonly known as cliques.

The basic definition of a clique is a small, exclusive group of people. But to most teenagers, cliques mean much more than that. As teens become more independent, friends often act as a family away from home. They provide support and acceptance and let you know that what you are thinking and feeling is OK. Becoming part of a clique is also a way of establishing your identity and defining who you are.

Despite these good points, cliques often make life very difficult for many teens. For everyone who feels like a secure part of a group, there is someone who feels left out and ignored.

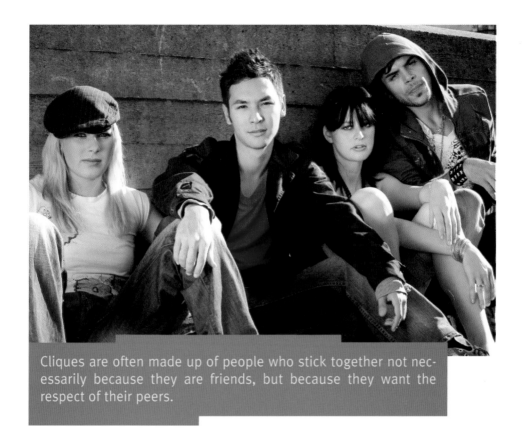

Cliques are often made up of people who stick together not necessarily because they are friends, but because they want the respect of their peers.

Relationships in cliques can be fickle. You may feel as if you don't know who your true friends are. You might hide parts of your personality in order to be accepted, or give up a certain goal or ambition that the group doesn't consider cool. Cliques have been shown, in films like *Heathers* and *Mean Girls*, as being exclusive, judgmental, and even cruel to outsiders. In these kinds of cliques, there is often a Queen Bee, or a girl leader of the group, who decides to target an outsider. This girl controls the attitudes and behaviors of the group, making a nice gathering of teens act mean. But this is not the only kind of Queen Bee and not the only kind of clique. Just like any groups of people, there can be negative cliques, but cliques are also positive social groups.

Whether you love cliques or hate them, they are probably going to be around as long as junior high and high school exist. Indeed, many experts feel that inclusion in a social group is an important part of growing up and helps prepare teens for life as adults.

If you don't belong to the most popular group, and then suddenly one of your friends gains acceptance into that crowd, this can make you feel rejected or that your friend would choose to be popular than choose to have real friendships. Or if you and your friends are part of a circle that likes to get together to play chess and somebody's new friend doesn't like to play chess, this can make you feel that your friendship is on shaky ground.

Some adults underestimate what teens go through and believe that they're shielded from the "real world" and that being concerned with social status isn't very important. When a teen worries about where he or she stands with cliques at school, the root of it may be a desire to be accepted and treated with respect and fairness. This is something that a friend finds difficult to understand, too, when another friend joins a different crowd. The hurt may be due to jealousy, or it may result as a feeling of abandonment.

This, too, is a common scenario. Realize that if your friend decides to pick popular friends over you, someone who has proven to be loyal, then your friendship would have most likely reached an expiration date anyway, whether or not your friend is part of a new clique at school. If your friend doesn't like chess as much as he or she used to, then he or she should not pretend to like it either. This doesn't mean that you guys can't be friends and have nothing in common. It just means you don't have chess in common.

Growing Apart

There is a growing apart that happens to neighborhood children who shared swing sets and grow up to have nothing in common. If shared memories are strong enough, or yours is a community in which neighbors stay friends, then you may remain friends as you grow up. Or you may just fall out of touch. As long as you want the same thing, there's no problem.

Changing at Different Speeds

This would be like growing apart, except one person feels it's time to move on and the other doesn't. By high school, you're going from being a teenager to an adult, perhaps on different schedules. If one person in a friendship wants change and the other doesn't, then one feels held back and the other feels abandoned.

Moving Apart

When a good friend moves, or you do, staying in touch can be hard. If you talked all the time and that's what you liked best,

As a young person, a move to a new place is likely your parents' doing and beyond your control. This may force you and your old friends to go in different directions.

you may be able to chat by phone or instant messaging instead. If the distances are great and you can't see each other often, you may find yourselves growing apart. It's easy for the person who moves to feel forgotten. It's easy for the person left behind to be threatened by news of new friends and interests. Staying friends requires letting each of you make new friends while still staying in touch. Some friends can be apart for a long time, and when they see each other again, they feel like they've never been apart. Others feel like strangers. Both situations are normal.

Getting Ditched

The easiest way to end a friendship is when both parties grow apart. The hardest is getting dumped suddenly by a friend.

When You Don't Know What Hit You

Friendships, even close ones, sometimes end without warning. You come back from summer vacation and your friends say, "We're not friends anymore." Your friend swears you did something terrible. You know you didn't do it, or you don't know what she is talking about and she won't tell you. Maybe there's a terrible fight. Maybe you're just cut out of his or her life—but it's over and there seems to be nothing you can do about it.

If you don't want to stop being friends, or you don't clearly understand what happened, here's what you can try:

- As calmly as possible, tell your friend that you'll miss him or her.
- Ask your friend to talk to you either in person or in an e-mail about what happened.

If You Did Something Very Wrong

Sometimes you know exactly why your friend wants to end the friendship. You know that you did something that was not nice. If this was an isolated incident, then you can seriously apologize, swear that you will never be so stupid again, and hope that he or she can forgive you. If what you did was hurtful enough, or if

Ironically, finding new friends sometimes requires spending time alone and thinking about the relationship mistakes you've made with past friends.

the friendship wasn't rock-solid to begin with, then apologizing may not be enough. You are going to have to grieve for the loss of the friendship. Try to get something out of this loss, however. Be introspective and make sure you learn your lesson about how to treat people. Also, know that everybody makes mistakes. What you did may not have been commendable, but you should be able to forgive yourself for it and move on.

CAN THIS FRIENDSHIP BE SAVED?

There are plenty of reasons why friendships land on the rocks, but they don't all have to sink. Friendships don't have to end. They can change or adjust, if that's what everyone wants. But that means you both have to care enough to be able to talk honestly about what's going on.

Insecurity

When a friend gets clingy, very competitive, or jealous, that's hard on the relationship. If your friend—or you—have gotten clingy, it's almost certainly because the clinger is feeling insecure and is worried that he or she will lose a friend. So if you push the clinger away, that's going to make it worse. Jealousy or competitiveness is also likely to come from insecurity. It may be hard to reassure someone who is annoying you, but if you want to keep the person as a friend, then that's what you're going to have to do. The person has to be able to believe you and change his or her behavior.

If you're feeling insecure and are acting needy toward your friend, then you should evaluate what is making you feel self-conscious and work on that. If you don't get to the root of your problems, you'll probably end up driving your friends away. In the meantime, keep your demands in check and give your friends their space.

Fights

People react differently to fighting. It depends on your family and your personality whether you feel "a good fight clears the air" and you breathe easier afterward, or whether you feel that a fight means people don't like one another and you have trouble breathing at all afterward. Some families yell and slam doors, and then yell, laugh, and eventually feel great. The anger is real anger, but letting it out helps them get over the anger. In another family, the anger may be poisonous. When people fight, they're really trying to hurt one another. Fighting doesn't let the anger out safely, it just makes the anger worse. It can be hard for someone raised in an environment similar to this to realize that a friend's anger may be intended to clear the air or that fighting can ever be healthy. It can be.

A healthy fight involves strong feelings and strong disagreement, but you're not actually trying to draw blood. You don't say things to hurt the other person, using your intimate knowledge

Fights between friends are often turning points in relationships. Your opinions surface and reveal whether you can live with your differences.

of him or her to do as much damage as possible. Ideally, the outcome of the fight is that you resolve the problem and stay friends. That means you need to listen to the other person and not just wait until she runs out of breath so that you can tell her how wrong she is.

If you started with an argument about what movie to go to and wound up yelling about bossiness, then you need to take a breather. You'll have to talk more quietly, maybe after some time has passed. Keep the argument related to the situation. Don't start polling other friends on the subject, because once other people are involved, the fight may become more serious and expand beyond the actual issue.

This remains true even if the fight has gotten ugly or is about something serious. Maybe there's been a great misunderstanding. Maybe one person has hurt the other (whether she meant to or not). Fights sometimes start because of jealousy. Or because someone is feeling lousy about something else entirely and took it out on the closest person to him—his friend.

Resolving the problem still involves listening carefully and expressing your point of view as clearly as you can—not to hurt the other person, but to figure out what happened and what you can both do about it. Focus on the matter at hand; don't bring up things that happened a few years ago. Use "I" statements such as "I felt terrible when you went to the party I wasn't invited to," rather than accusations starting with "you never" or "you shouldn't." Try to find a solution with which you can both live, that will help avoid future fights on the same subject. Learn to fight fairly, and learn to compromise.

Lost in the Tunnel of Love

You may have a friend who has fallen in love and has not been heard from since—or can talk only about the new sweetie. There are also people who are always falling in love and are available only between romances. It's true that the intensity of a new romance can make the rest of the world look dim by comparison. Still, high school romances tend to burn out faster than friendships do, and neglecting friends for a romance isn't healthy.

If your friend has vanished into a romance, suggest you plan some friends-only time together. If your friend is really lost to you right now, at least stop being surprised. Make other plans. If this is a friend who makes a habit of fleeing into romances, then he or she seriously needs not to be your only friend. You'll have to decide, and let the other person know, whether you feel he or she is worth the patience. It may be that you are delighted to have her around, when she can be, or that you simply find it too painful to be picked up or dropped depending on whether she has anything better to do. That will really depend on how you feel about it. When evaluating whether your friend is worth it or not, be honest about what you should mean to somebody. Don't sell yourself short by holding on to a person who doesn't actually make a very good friend or value that you make a good friend.

Making It Known

We often become friends with people because we're alike in some important way and different in other ways. You may have

Having friends who have different interests and talents can be a good thing. These differences, however, should be celebrated and not abused.

always gotten along great with a friend because he or she likes to plan things (and is maybe a little bossy) and you like to do things, but don't like to plan them. That's fine—until the other person wonders why he or she always has to plan everything.

If someone feels taken advantage of or has just gotten tired of playing the role she's always played, she has to tell you. She shouldn't assume that her friends will be able to read her mind or that acting grumpy about it will show that she wants things to change.

All Sorts of Other Changes

There is a long list of ways people can change. None is absolutely a reason to end a friendship if the friends still care about each other.

If one of you is interested in being romantic partners and the other isn't, see if the feelings of friendship are strong enough to make the friendship worth saving. Perhaps all you need is to take a break from each other. Also, if your friend rejects you, try not to take this too personally. He or she liked you enough to build a friendship with you, but a romance is a lot different from a friendship.

If your groups of friends don't get along or have come to disagree strongly about some things, you can probably still be friends. Agree not to talk about politics or each other's taste in romantic partners, and do something that everyone enjoys. Go to the movies, and talk about the movie. Share whatever it is that still ties you together and agree to disagree about the rest. That's not dishonest—it's good practice for adult life because you're not going to like everything about the people with whom you work or all your spouse's friends and interests.

When It's Time for You to End a Friendship

You try to talk honestly with your friend to fix a problem, but it doesn't help. If your friend is doing any of the following, it might be time to evaluate whether or not a friendship is worth the work:

If you realize that your friendship with someone is not healthy, the best way to end it is to have a mature conversation, not an emotional separation.

➤ Your friend is mean and is always "telling you this for your own good," but you're pretty sure she just likes putting you down. She says you're lucky to have her because no one else would want you for a friend. Therefore, it's OK if she mocks you, puts you down, or otherwise hurts you. It's not.

➤ Your friend often tells secrets you've entrusted him with, or gossips about you behind your back.

➤ Your friend acts like she owns you. It's futile to persuade her to relax or for her to believe that you can be friends and still have other friends.

➤ Your friend competes with you. He has to go out with the person you like, objects to you ever doing better on a test, or even has to top any problem you have with a bigger one. A little competition can be healthy and normal, but if someone always has to win, then he's not respecting your friendship or you.

➤ Your friend always wants to talk and never wants to listen.

➤ Your friend always has to be right about everything. Not just someone with strong opinions who likes to argue, but someone whose attitude is "my way or the highway."

➤ Your friend pressures you to take drugs or engage in illegal activities, or insists that you do things you deeply don't want to do. This does not include going to her boring piano recital, but it does include dangerous activities such as driving too fast, climbing fences with signs that say DANGER: HIGH VOLTAGE, or any other behavior that seems like a bad idea.

When a friend pressures you to do things you don't want to do, it's time to question whether the friendship is worth preserving.

The obvious problem here is the danger. It's also your friend's lack of respect for what you want or think. Keeping a friend who says or shows that she won't be your friend unless you do what she says is as crazy as letting somebody else control your life.

Even if you don't understand how he does it, your friend makes you feel lousy or used when you're with him. If you feel as though you have to be fake to get along with him or you just get on each other's nerves all the time, it's probably time to be honest with yourself (and with him).

How to End a Friendship

If you can, be honest with your friend about why you are ending it. Not "You're horrible, and I don't want to be your friend anymore," but some version of the truth that won't devastate the person with whom you've spent a considerable portion of your free time. Most people really aren't horrible in their hearts. There is no need to hurt them. If you suspect this person might truly be horrible in his or her heart, then there's no point in making that person furious. If you can't confront your friend directly, it may be possible to simply become less available. Make other plans and see if you can part gradually, without an uproar.

chapter four

HOW DO I MOVE ON?

What can you do if you've lost your friends, or you've moved somewhere new and don't know anyone? What if your ex-friends say, "Get a life," and after thinking about it, you realize, "Maybe they're right?" If you've looked to the same friend or small group of friends to fulfill all your needs, it might be true that your social circle is too small. People vary in how many friends and activities they want and need, but maybe you need to broaden your interests. After all, friendship is a big part of your life, but it's not your whole life.

The Loss of a Friend

Your friend may not want or be able to tell you what happened. You may never know, and there's nothing you can do about it. If this is someone you have trusted and even loved for years, it is hideously painful. It is like the sort of betrayal people feel when a romance of many years collapses, and one partner didn't see it coming. As with other terrible losses in life, you can only try to get through it as best you can.

What Not to Do

First thing, try not to cling, beg, become abusive, or attempt to make the dumper feel guilty. It won't help, and you will feel worse afterward. You might just want to occupy yourself with your other friends, by doing things alone, or by letting it out and crying if you need it. If there's any possibility that your friend has gone through some temporary lunacy, you may want to leave the door open to being friends in the future.

Hard as it might be, try not to take it too personally or blame yourself excessively. If you've been abandoned for no apparent reason, this may seem like the perfect time to get down on yourself, but it's not. If you have just been deeply hurt by someone you care about, you don't have enough perspective right now to decide if it's a time to make big changes in your life. Wait until you are not in mourning. In the meantime, avoid any version of "No one likes me" and "I'm a loser" by surrounding yourself with people who you know like you, like your family or other friends. Immerse yourself in activities that make you happy, and try to keep the end of your friendship in perspective.

Try to refrain from spending too much time figuring out who was at fault for the breakup. Of course, you're going to think about what happened and wonder if the outcome could have been different. If the breakup was sudden and your friend

After a friendship ends, the best way to deal with your emotions is to take pause and collect your thoughts.

won't talk to you about it, there's not much you'll be able to figure out.

Lastly, try not to bad-mouth your ex-friend to anyone who will listen. That just makes you look bad. Try to be compassionate toward your ex-friend. The teen years are a time of tremendous growth and change, and nobody but he or she knows exactly what is going on inside him or her. Keep in mind that you guys had good experiences, and let this serve as a reminder that stops you from seeking revenge.

What to Do

When a friend rejects you, you have lost two things: the friend, and a part of yourself. It's painful. Allow yourself to grieve.

Someone is sure to say, "Well, you don't want to be friends with someone who would do that"—whatever "that" is. Actually, you may feel that you do. He or she was your friend. No matter what happened, you may feel for a while that all you want is for your friend to want to be with you again. Trust that in time, that feeling will not be so intense. Believe that you will have other friends and will feel better.

You might feel like hiding under the bed, but hold on to your regular routine as much as possible. Go to class, after-school clubs, work, and join family activities. Your routine will keep you busy while time begins to heal you. They are also sources to make new friends.

Remember to get support for yourself during this time. Talk to trusted family members, perhaps a cousin or aunt or uncle if

Though spending time with yourself may be healthy after a friendship ends, try to avoid becoming a person who stays alone all of the time.

you're not comfortable talking with your parents. Catch up with your long-distance friendships if you have some. Don't stay isolated with your pain because that will make it worse.

Find Yourself

If you've moved somewhere new or just lost your friends, it's time to think about who you are and what you like to do. If you're naturally outgoing and happy to approach strangers to chat, then you are likely to wind up with a wide circle of friends.

Myths and Facts

About When a Friendship Ends

Close friends never fight. Fact ➡ Some close friends fight occasionally. Others prefer a calmer relationship and have other ways of addressing problems. Both are fine, as long as you and your friend have some way of getting problems into the open so they can be talked about and resolved.

Real friends stay friends forever. Fact ➡ You will have different friends during different times in your life, and very few will be lifelong friends. Losing friendships is a natural part of living life.

Myth: Friends keep each other's secrets, no matter what. Fact ➡ Friendship may require you to keep quiet about things that you'd rather talk about. Friendship requires you to judge, very carefully, whether a secret needs to be shared to keep your friend safe. When someone is being physically or sexually abused, is hurting themselves (cutting), is threatening suicide, or is collecting firearms and talking about bringing them to school, those are the types of secrets that you shouldn't keep. You have to notify someone who can help. However, you should never tell on your friend because you disapprove or are jealous of him or her. A good rule of thumb is to ask yourself if you're tattling for his or her safety or because you're annoyed.

Real friends are like twins—they agree about nearly everything and even know what the other is thinking.

Fact ➡ Some people have very twin-like friendships, even dressing alike when they're little. It can be startling and wonderful to find a friend who knows you so well that you can finish each other's thoughts. However, these close friendships can become stifling as you develop your own interests. Differences can be almost as important as similarities in a friendship. Real friends both compliment and complement one another. What's important in a friendship is not only that you can read each other's minds, but also that you can speak your own mind.

If that seems rather daunting, try something else: do the things you like to do anyway. Find team sports, book discussion groups, art classes, or a group with whom to play a musical instrument. Volunteer by tutoring kids in computers. Whatever you like to do, do it.

Taking part in various community activities, such as volunteer work, is a great way to discover your interests and friends with similar likings.

Don't limit yourself to school groups. See what the church, synagogue, mosque, YMCA, or neighborhood association has to offer. Or see what you could offer them. Try something new. If you've been hurt by people and like animals, go work at the animal shelter. Animals can be good company, too.

There are probably friends for you in these places, and they will be people who like doing something you like. In the meantime, just enjoy the activities. This is a more active and fun way of looking for friends. It beats looking sadly around the school cafeteria wishing someone would talk to you, or trying to dress and act a certain way, hoping that a particular clique will take you in. If you're doing something you enjoy with other people who enjoy it, too, you're more likely to be comfortable and naturally friendly. You have the activity in common, so you're not trying to make conversation out of thin air.

Your Life

In short, if you're new in town or are between friends, it's time for you to see what you enjoy doing, whether or not you're doing it with others. Do the stuff you're responsible for, like schoolwork, family obligations, and a part-time job. Push yourself a little. Go to a movie alone, just to enjoy the movie. Take a walk by yourself and think your own thoughts and see what the world looks like to you when there's no one to tell you how to think about it. Do anything you think might be interesting, especially if it's something your ex-friends would have said is stupid. Do it because you want to.

There is an endless number of people with whom you can be friends. There's no reason why you need to be stuck in an unhealthy friendship.

Human beings are social creatures. We like to be with others. If you learn to be comfortable by yourself and have your own interests, then you bring more to your relationships with other people. If you are totally uncomfortable being alone, then you may find yourself settling for anyone who will hang with you. If you feel you have no control over who is in your life, this might not bode well for your feelings of self-worth. If you have your own interests and enjoy your own company, then you can be choosy. Hold out for real friends—casual friends you've met at some of your activities and close friends who may turn up when you least expect them.

HOW DO I MAKE NEW FRIENDS?

Leaving a group of friends, even if it is the right thing to do, is very difficult. There is comfort and security in staying with people you already know and who already know you. Depending on your reasons for leaving, you may still be able to do things with your old group of friends while trying to make new friends. If you feel you need a complete break, there may be a period of loneliness as you feel out other people and as they get to know you. Remember that good friendships are based on trust, and that is something that can only be gained over time.

Relax!

One reason people find it difficult to make friends is because they fear rejection. Many are so afraid of being

You don't always have to approach new people to make friends. Simply smile and have a welcoming attitude, and people will seek your company.

turned away that they don't even try to become friends with people they admire and would like to get to know better. So, the first step in making new friends is to relax and realize that everyone else feels the same way. Even people who seem as if they have great friends may worry that someone new won't like them.

Be Approachable

If you are always surrounded by the same group of friends, it will seem as if you aren't trying to meet new people and others will stay away. If you give off signals that you don't want to be disturbed, such as never making eye contact or keeping your head down when walking through the halls, people won't try to talk to you. To look like you are interested in meeting someone, catch his or her eye and smile.

You should also try to talk with him or her. This doesn't mean you have to blurt out a major statement like, "Hi, I think you are nice and would like to be your friend." It can be as simple as walking out of math class with someone and asking, "Did you understand that last problem?" It isn't easy, but if you take the first steps, you may find a wonderful new group of friends.

Get Involved

Another way to meet new people is to take part in an activity or group that seems interesting. It could be something organized

1 In a 2004 poll, 37 percent of people between fifteen and twenty-nine years old reported that they had more than five close friends; 85 percent said they had more than five other friends; and almost 11 percent had at least five acquaintances, too.

2 The first Sunday in August is National Friendship Day in the United States. It was established by Congress in 1935.

3 An old proverb says, "You can choose your friends, but you can't choose your relatives."

4 According to a 2001 Canadian survey, almost 40 percent of males ages fifteen to nineteen and 50 percent of teen girls worry about losing their friends.

5 The more friends women have, the less likely they are to develop physical impairments as they age.

6 Nineteenth-century writer Ralph Waldo Emerson is famous for saying, "The only way to have a friend is to be a friend." He also said, "It is one of the blessings of old friends that you can afford to be stupid with them."

7 The seventeenth-century English poet George Herbert said, "The best mirror is an old friend."

8 In Italian, a best friend is called *amica del cuore*, which translates literally into "friend of the heart."

9 Teen friendships are usually a lot longer-lasting than romances.

10 Fighting between friends isn't always a bad thing. Sometimes it's healthy to express anger.

at school, such as a theater group, debate club, or yearbook committee. Or it could be something outside of school, such as a part-time job or a volunteer activity.

There are many benefits to meeting people in this kind of setting. One is that you know you already have one thing in common—the interest in the activity. Another is that it automatically gives you something to talk about. Third, it is easy to have these activities lead to other things. For instance, if you are in the drama club, you will probably have rehearsals after school. It would be much easier to ask people to go out to eat after rehearsal than if you only saw them during the school day.

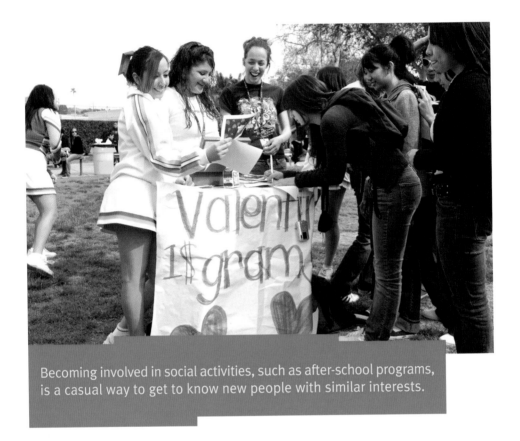

Becoming involved in social activities, such as after-school programs, is a casual way to get to know new people with similar interests.

Here is a list of ideas about things to do to help you make new friends:

- Say hi to people when you pass them in the hall.
- When someone talks to you, focus on him or her.
- Join a club or team that interests you.
- Make sure your body language is open and friendly.
- Don't judge people on their outward appearances.
- Don't gossip.

accusation Statement that somebody has done something wrong or inappropriate.

betrayal An act of failing someone. It can also mean the act of turning someone over to an enemy.

complement Something that fills up or completes something (or someone).

conflict The struggles that result when different people want different things.

devastate To bring to hopelessness, chaos, or despair.

discretion The ability to know when to speak or not to speak of something.

excessive Too much; more than is reasonable.

gossip Rumors or reports about other people and their activities, especially when these are things the people might want kept private.

love Strong affection, warm attachment, unselfish devotion, and tenderness toward somebody or something.

mutual A shared feeling or opinion.

perspective The ability to keep track of the true importance of something; not losing sight of the whole picture.

American Psychological Association Help Center
750 First Street NE
Washington, DC 20002-4242
(800) 374-2721
Web site: http://www.helping.apa.org
  APA's Help Center is an online resource about psychological
  issues that affect physical and emotional well-being. It also
  provides referrals to counselors.

National Institutes of Health
MedlinePlus
8600 Rockville Pike
Bethesda, MD 20894
Web site: http://www.nlm.nih.gov/medlineplus/
  teenmentalhealth.html
  MedlinePlus is a resource that addresses the mental
  health issues of young people, including teen suicide and
  the ending of friendships.

The Ophelia Project
718 Nevada Drive
Erie, PA 16505
(888) 256-KIDS (5437)
Web site: http://www.opheliaproject.org

The Ophelia Project is a nonprofit organization that advocates teen issues, particularly those that teen girls face.

TeenHelp.org
Web site: http://www.teenhelp.org
TeenHelp.org is dedicated to giving advice to teens. With more than 25,000 teen members, it offers a support forum and counsel from more than 100 e-mail mentors.

Teen Line
Cedars-Sinai Medical Center
P.O. Box 48750
Los Angeles, CA 90048
(310) 855-4673 (HOPE)
Web site: http://www.teenlineonline.org
Teen Line offers support on the issues people face while growing up. Teens who need to talk are encouraged to call the hotline, which is open from 6 PM to 10 PM (PST).

TeenScreen
Columbia University
2960 Broadway
New York, NY 10027-6902
(866) 833-6727
E-mail: teenscreen@childpsych.columbia.edu
Web site: http://www.teenscreen.org/index.htm
TeenScreen, a branch of Columbia University, is an organization dedicated to monitoring the mental health of young people.

TeensHealth.org

Web site: http://www.teenshealth.org/teen

TeensHealth.org is a Web site that offers advice on a variety of emotional issues.

YMCA of the USA

101 North Wacker Drive

Chicago, IL 60606

(312) 977-0031

Web site: http://www.ymca.net

YMCA offers counseling and coping resources, as well as activities for youths.

Web Sites

Due to the changing nature of Internet links, Rosen Publishing has developed an online list of Web sites related to the subject of this book. This site is updated regularly. Please use this link to access the list:

http://www.rosenlinks.com/faq/whfe

For Further Reading

Canfield, Jack, and Mark Victor Hansen. *Chicken Soup for the Teenage Soul on Love & Friendship.* Deerfield Beach, FL: Health Communications, 2002.

Carnegie, Dale. *How to Win Friends & Influence People.* New York, NY: Pocket, 1990.

Carnegie, Donna Dale. *How to Win Friends and Influence People for Teen Girls.* New York, NY: Fireside, 2005.

Clement, Claude. *Don't Be Shy: How to Fit in, Make Friends, and Have Fun—Even If You Weren't Born Outgoing.* London, UK: Amulet Books, 2005.

Cohen-Posey, Kate. *How to Handle Bullies, Teasers, and Other Meanies: A Book That Takes the Nuisance Out of Name Calling and Other Nonsense.* Lake Zurich, IL: Rainbow Books, 1995.

Davis, Sampson. *We Beat the Street: How a Friendship Pact Led to Success.* New York, NY: Puffin, 2006.

Desetta, Al (editor). *The Courage to Be Yourself: True Stories by Teens About Cliques, Conflicts, and Overcoming Peer Pressure.* Minneapolis, MN: Free Spirit, 2005.

Frankel, Fred. *Good Friends Are Hard to Find: Help Your Child Find, Make, and Keep Friends.* London, UK: Perspective Publishing, 1996.

Gabor, Don. *How to Start a Conversation and Make Friends.* New York, NY: Fireside, 2001.

Kaufman, Gershen. *Stick Up for Yourself: Every Kid's Guide to Personal Power & Positive Self-Esteem.* Minneapolis, MN: Free Spirit Publishing, 1999.

Kirberger, Kimberly. *On Friendship: A Book for Teenagers.* Deerfield Beach, FL: Health Communications, 2000.

Lutz, Ericka. *The Complete Idiot's Guide to Friendship for Teens.* Indianapolis, IN: Alpha Books, 2001.

Michelle, Lonny. *How Kids Make Friends: Secrets for Making Lots of Friends, No Matter How Shy You Are.* Evanston, IL: Freedom Publishing Company, 1997.

Musgrove, Susan. *You Be Me: Friendship in the Lives of Teen Girls.* New York, NY: Annick Press, 2002.

Romain, Trevor. *Cliques, Phonies, & Other Baloney.* Minneapolis, MN: Free Spirit Publishing, 1998.

Shaw, Victoria. *Best Buds: A Girl's Guide to Friendship.* New York, NY: Rosen Central, 2000.

Bibliography

Hey, Valerie. *The Company She Keeps: An Ethnography of Girls' Friendships.* London, UK: Open University Press, 1997.

Lutz, Ericka. *The Complete Idiot's Guide to Friendship for Teens.* Indianapolis, IN: Alpha Books, 2001.

Spencer, Liz, and Ray Pahl. *Rethinking Friendship: Hidden Solidarities Today.* Princeton, NJ: Princeton University Press, 2006.

Taylor, S. E., *et al.* "Female Response to Stress: Tend-and-Befriend, Not Fight-or-Flight." *Psychological Review* 107 (3), 411–429, 2000.

Yager, Jan. *When Friendship Hurts: How to Deal with Friends Who Betray, Abandon, or Wound You.* New York, NY: Simon & Schuster, 2002.

Index

Photo Credits

Designer: Tahara Anderson; **Editor:** Nicholas Croce
Photo Researcher: Amy Feinberg